O, Heart
Claudia Keelan

O, Heart
Claudia Keelan

Barrow Street Press
New York City

© 2014 by Claudia Keelan
All rights reserved

Designed by Robert Drummond
Cover design by Robert Drummond
Cover Illustration by Diana Cundall, Cleveland, OH

Published by Barrow Street Press
Distributed by:
    Barrow Street Books
    P.O. Box 1558
    Kingston, RI 02881

First Edition

Library of Congress Control Number: 2014936593

ISBN 978-0-9893296-2-0

*Dedicated to
Lona Alice Keelan*

CONTENTS

O, Heart
1. Empire   3
Primary Directive   4
Primary Directive 2   6
First Acts   8
Mothers Medley   10
Shaky Girls   11
Scene 4   12
Scene 4, Act 2   14
Second Acts   16
Coda   18
Scene 4, Act 3   19
Shaky Girls 2   21
Shaky Girls 3   22
Voice-over   23
Cast   24
King Heart   26
Scene 5   27
Mojave Letter   30
Scene 6   33
Apology   36
Dark Comedy   37
Agape, The Woman Is Agape   38
Continuous Acts   39

Eternal Direction / Insurrection	51
Continuous Acts	52
(HIS)torical Heart	57
Scene 7	58
The Practical Fruit, Some Small Piece of It	60
Mojave Letter	61
Leonardo, Leonardo	62
Agape, The Woman Is Agape	63
Retrograde Heart	64

Acknowledgments

O, Heart

1. Empire

It was, the vision men kept telling her, only an organ

Only a vessel that provided blood

It was a telltale, a changed, a rent

"In an average lifetime, the heart beats more than two and a half billion times, without ever pausing to rest."

The open heart the opened heart's

"... life-sustaining power has, throughout time, caused an air of mystery to surround it..."

Primary Directive

The woman is alone on stage

She is next to a tree

Then on top of the water, a huge dress floating

Yes, the woman is alone with herself on the stage

She is looking towards something we cannot see,
You cannot see, watching her

It is her life, and it is there, in sequence, in a slide
Show, before her eyes behind

Her eyes—We cannot see

First, there was a dollhouse, it was not hers

Second, the two thumbs her own and oh, so soon,

A figure that loves her who is standing over her talking

The woman looks reflective, amused even,
And her hands move like speech

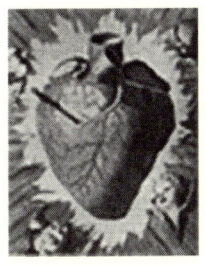
"The heart, as Master Nicolaus had aptly observed in the late twelfth century, was the primary 'spiritual member' of the body…"

Harvey described the heart as the "king" or "sun" of the body to underscore its cosmological significance.

"If indeed from the heart alone rise anger or passion, fear, terror, and sadness; if from it alone spring shame, delight, and joy, why should I say more?"

—Andreas de Laguna (1535)

Primary Directive 2

Once, there was a woman much as she,
Turning her eyes, pointing with her eyes,
At the stranger who lived in their home.
Turning with her eyes, pointing with her eyes,
Turning and pointing without words
Her look begged: "love him."

No. The woman is alone.
This woman was not as she.
Her stranger is not her stranger.

Father, on the beach, is it?

Stranger, with my hands around your neck, is it?

Alone on the stage,
She is surrounded by violins
And they play through her
As she hurries stage right
Stage left with them
And with the beating of her own heart

There was a prior story
Prior to this newest singularity

There was a prior
There is always a prior
A priori it is the *a priori*
She seeks now
Looking from stranger
To stranger to see

How it had come, his looking at,
Without seeing, her,
The real blank of it,
The real black portion in the eye
Something stripped out,
Something really not there anymore

First Acts

The woman is alone on the stage

"His eye would trouble me no more..."

What was in Poe's heart
That all his tales express the outward
Murder or death of something—

Old men, eyes, Ligeia, hearts, etc—
While the narrator goes quickly crazy himself,
Embodied and disembodied, in the act?

"Meantime the hellish tattoo of the heart increased..."

And no one can tell if it's his
Or the old man's, though it becomes clear—
Nothing becomes clear.

In the 19th century,
People believed that emotions
Came from the heart
But now we know
That they come from the brain—
Emotions, and that helps us to—

Ahab and his whale,
Hawthorne and "The Birthmark"
And *The Scarlet Letter*,
All these signs signifying

The Red Badge of Courage

Every girl loves a coward

Edna swimming out to sea
At the end of *The Awakening*,
Swimming away from possession,
Swimming into the possession
Of her own heart,
Which drowns her

Mothers Medley

"Oh, I'm burning! I wish I were out of doors! I wish I were a girl again, half savage and hardy, and free; and laughing at injuries, not maddening under them! Why am I so changed?"
—Emily Brontë

Oh and dear sister, Jane Bowles,
loving Paul, loving her sisters,
laughing all the way to her grave:

"At this moment Mrs. Copperfield was…reminded of a dream that had recurred often during her life…she was being chased up a short hill by a dog. At the top of the hill there stood… a mannequin about eight feet high…She approached the mannequin and discovered her to be fashioned out of flesh, but without life…Mrs. Copperfield wrapped one of the mannequin's arms tightly about her own waist…Then the mannequin began to sway backwards and forward…and together they fell off the top of the hill and continued rolling for quite a distance until they landed…where they remained locked in each others arms."
—Jane Bowles

Shaky Girls

"O, break my heart! poor bankrupt, break at once!"

To prison, eyes

She is flipping through the tragedies, stopped now,
Holding a large book

Sing willow

Scene 4

Alone on the stage,
She is directed to consider
The ways in which the heart
—not the organ, well yes, in part the organ,
But in part the other,
The mystery that is the heart
—is reflected in the eyes.

Uncertain

Though we cannot see what she sees,
And what comes to us, the watching ones,
Is always partial, we see her looking
Now and what she sees

First, a dollhouse, it's not hers
But she sees it through the slats of a crib,
It is green and her sister's,
Two stories and tiny figures
Eat and sleep throughout it

They took away her thumbs

So soon a stranger standing talking

Direction: why allow?

Stand up stand beside
Make your heart a fist

But music, the music,
She hears it above all
And it swells through her,
With her, and the violins summon
Her pity and expectation

Trumpets?

Entry.

And she likes them?

Sometimes.

Scene 4, Act 2

"Occitania alone produced women troubadours
…the women's language is in every sense, new…"

Her heart is a violin
Loving her stranger

It is the shape of a flame,
A tongue and it reaches—

The violin loves her,
It is a shape,
A whole shape:
It is pity

Stop it

The violin loves her
It is a shape,
It is a tongue,
It is a movement towards

Are you looking at her?
Can you see what is in her eyes?

She is alone,
Holding a violin,
Cradling a violin
In the bend of her elbow

It is crying,
She is crying,
And feeding it
From her mouth

A clearing opens up around them
There is a sound
A sound   is it peace

Some worry and some more

She is bending and bowing
Bending and bowing
And the violin's notes
Turn upward turn away
And through the clearing,
Their clearing, the woman
And the sound she is making

  They are so happy,
  Going nowhere,
  They are so happy,
  Leaning into nowhere.
  Please never let it stop—
  Please never let it stop—
  Please never let it—
  This sound this movement moving

Second Acts

She is standing alone on the stage
And the empty space conspires with her

Emptiness conspiring with the various
Strains the violin threads through
—her heart?

"Now we are come to the cold time
When the ice and snow and the mud
And the birds' beaks are mute
(For not one inclines to sing);
And the hedge branches are dry—
No leaf nor bud sprouts up,
Nor cries the nightingale
Whose song awakens me in May."

She is looking out past you
She is seeing a woman
She thinks is herself
Alone at a desk

She sees her often
Sitting at a desk
Sitting at a desk by a window
There are trees
It is dark

She wonders if she has ever
Really seen her
The woman she thinks is herself
Sitting at a desk with windows and trees

If she cannot be sure she has seen her
The woman desk-window-trees
If she cannot be sure
This sight is sight
Then why should you want
Her questionable picture?

The woman is a sound,
A movement towards a conclusion.
A present and visible memory
Of a sound and a shape, that seems true to her.

Coda

Working working workingworkingworking
Work work work work
Beingbeingbeingbeingbeingbeingbeing
BE BE BE BE
Workingworkingworkingworkingworking
Being
Work
Being
Work
Be

Scene 4, Act 3

Direction: ditch emotion

Why?

Ditch it

Why?

The violin is tiptoeing
What does it fear

The violin is tiptoeing
Without fear

It is shirking the opening
The stranger
The woman

"Of things I'd rather keep in silence I must sing"

Shirk shirk

The violin is conspiring
With the plenty

The horns are there too,
Watch the swelling
It is emotion, which is why
The composer flattens it,
Flattens it to balance
The empty with the plenty

All that triumphalism and conclusion

Stupid horn,
Stupid galloping,
Stupid triumph

All of this is something the woman found
Via her organ, a heart,
A shape
A sound
A movement towards
And away from a house
And stranger
A song played between
The empty and plenty
One woman and her other

All this is something
Visibly invisible in the eye

"So I send you, there on your estate
This song as messenger and delegate…"

Shaky Girls 2

"You are a spirit I know. Where did you die?"

Shaky Girls 3

"You are a spirit I know. Where did you die?"

She is flipping through the tragedies, stopped now,
Holding a large book.

Voice-over

Because I am going to die
I wonder at the models

Killing others to find
You've ended your own life

Swimming solo with your own heart
Until you can't keep going anymore?

Emily Dickinson begs the question

As does Emily Brontë
Really all of the Brontë sisters

And Hawthorne's really large heart
In Hester Prynne, her loyalty
To an absent minister,
Her devotion to invisibility,
Her charity

Xenobia is Hester outed,
A visible model of progressive womanhood
And her submission to Hollingsworth's
Utopian ideals make her trivial,
As is anyone in search
Of a consensual answer

The woman's heart keeps rising
To something she can't see

Cast

O, HEART: A DRAMA, BOTH "CLOSET" AND VERSE

SHE: SOMETIMES KNOWN AS "THE WOMAN"

HE: REFERED TO AS "THE STRANGER'"

THE HEART: THE ORGAN AND THE ENTITY, 'THE KING' AS PERCEIVED VIA STRUCTURES HISTORICAL, SCIENTIFIC, MUSICAL, LITERARY AND OTHERS

THE EYE: WHAT IT SEES, WHAT IT CAN'T, HOW IT FAILS OR SUCCEEDS IN REVEALING _____

LYRIC: SELF-REFERENTALITY, A PRETTY SONG DYING IN ITS OWN CHORDS

CORDELIA: A SPEECH AND A FIGURE TOWARDS HEART'S END

THE EAR: ITS VIRTUE, ITS AVAILABILITY AND INABILITY TO KEEP OUT, OR DISCRIMINATE

JANE BOWLES: SISTER TROPE

WILLIAM HARVEY: FATHER HEART

HESTER PRYNNE: ANGEL TROPE

HYSTERIA: THE TRUTH AVAILABLE IN HER, NOT TO BE CONFUSED WITH "SHE" OR "THE WOMAN"

POE: ANTITHETICAL MAN OR THE AUTHOR'S AVERSION TO THE BAROQUE

KATE CHOPIN: TROPE OF RESCUE

EMILY DICKINSON: SOLO TROPE

EMILY BRONTË: ANTITHETICAL WOMAN OR THE AUTHOR'S AVERSION TO THE LITERATURE OF OBSESSION

PITY: A CHRISTIAN IMPULSE, A SORROW, A MANNEQUIN

King Heart

"The play's the thing / Wherein I'll catch the conscience of the King."

Scene 5

Any listening room in the world. Pity is there, reading The Scarlet Letter *aloud to Jane Bowles and The Woman, who are drinking, who have been drinking, for hours. There are books all over the room, some open face down, all with paper clips serving as bookmarks. The Stranger looks through the window, flanked by William Harvey, stethoscope on The Stranger's heart, looking puzzled. Lyric poetry circles in a ticker tape over the borders of the room, which they read in fits and starts, shouting, like brokers on the floor of the stock market.*

Pity: "The child could not be made amenable to rules. In giving her existence, a great law had been broken; and the result was a being, whose elements were perhaps beautiful and brilliant, but all in disorder; or with an order peculiar to themselves, amidst which the point of variety and arrangement was difficult or impossible to be discovered."

Jane Bowles (*after a deep drink*): My own baby girl. Or me.

The Woman: No, just Pearl. Who could be most any, free, little girl. Yet still, a character in a novel, the nemesis of Beauty, that culture diva, and thus a new form whose direction is forward (*stops, pointing to the ticker tape, begins to recite, laughing so hard her drink comes out her nose*):
>Whenas in silks, my Julia goes,
> Then, then, methinks, how sweetly flows
> That liquefaction of her clothes…

Pity: I hate you two! (*throwing the Hawthorne novel on the floor she stomps out of the room*)

The Woman: You would! Who needs a Pity party anyway?

Jane Bowles: (*picking up the book Pity has left behind, reads*): "Throughout all, however, there was a trait of passion, a certain depth of hue, which she never lost; and if, in any of her changes, she had grown fainter or paler, she would have ceased to be herself—it would have been no longer Pearl!"

The Woman: Li-que-fac-tion. Let it flow!

Outside, William Harvey bangs on the window, but the women don't hear him, only a slight beating they think are moths against the pane. He uses his stethoscope like a microphone and reads from his treatise on the circulation of the blood, the De Motu Cordis.

Harvey: "The right and left sides of the heart work together, causing blood to flow continuously to the heart, lungs, and body.

Jane Bowles (*hand to her heart*): My sister!

Harvey (*reading*): "It is helpful to visualize the heart as two separate pumps,

Working in series—Right heart pump, left heart pump.

The heart has four chambers,

Two are muscular chambers that propel blood.

Two hold the blood

Returning to the heart and at just the right moment, empty."

Jane Bowles (*looking into her empty glass, nodding, shouts*): Empty!

Pity (*returning grumpily*): I know you think I'm done, but you need me.

Jane Bowles and The Woman speak, almost at once:

Jane Bowles: I wrote you, and replaced you with love.

The Woman: I became you and died.
(*Enter Emily Dickinson*)

Emily Dickinson: I heard a fly buzz when I died. You two really need to get a room.

The Woman (*reading from the ticker tape*): I celebrate myself, and sing myself / and what I assume, you shall assume.

Jane Bowles: Jeez.

William Harvey: Apocrypha!

Emily Dickinson: And you wonder why I never left home!

The Woman (*reading from the ticker tape*):
    I'm learning to hold myself
    The way I wanted you, or anyone
    To hold me, and see, I don't even need
    A mannequin to break my fall.
    I'm authentic
    I break my heart all by myself.

William Harvey: Interesting. I wonder if it's true.

Jane Bowles: It's true.

Emily Dickinson: It's unimportant. This world is not conclusion.

William Harvey: Obviously.

End of scene

Mojave Letter

They had come to a crossroads,
No, they had come to a juncture,
A split place,

Where light was shining still,
Though they were not
In the sun, shining, or so it seemed, now

Though the sun
Had been omnipresent,
They'd been under it for many years
& one day

She saw there was a weed, a long weed,
A mean and barbed thing
Poking from her side.
What a sad passage.

How had it come to be there, green
And twisted, low-lying and tenacious,
Stuck in her at an angle.

He, and she, we
The inconstant ones,
Though Auden's limestone was not their earth.

The issue in the split,
The issue in the juncture
And under the sun, with weed,

Was how to love there,
How to love now that
The beautiful boy had grown,

Auden's beautiful boy and ours.
Once I would have said the Christ child,
But our son bore no resemblance to that static star,
And I could see, could you?

The suffering boy who, almost grown,
Had come to know his resting place
Was not, as it had always been,

In his mother's arms. The boy glanced with side,
And then fully open, eyes at his father,
Who was gone now.

What is a man, what is a woman,
What are we now our Eros is wandering away,
Shuffling without form anymore
Save sympathy, save its body
In the shape of our son?

I stood beside, I touched
Her, she was a woman,
She loved us and she was calling our names.
She was older and tired,
But she was still standing
And she was calling us.

I must have lifted my eyes a dozen times,
Expecting you to come walking,
So fast as you do,
To appear suddenly at the corner,

Expecting again to lift
My eyes to meet yours,
Our story of us intact,

Pulling her, reaching through
Our Eros, to us.
I held her, waiting for you.

What can you tell me, poem,
About my stranger?

Is he safe,
Are they nice to him there,

Will you send him this weed,
The one I found growing in me,
This landscape
That is our whole life together?

Scene 6

Outside the window, the stranger is lying on the ground, looking at the stars. Pre-Raphaelite moths make a heart pattern around his cerebral cortex. He picks up the stethoscope Harvey has left behind and places it on his temple. He hears nothing, but sees behind his eyes the French statue of Liberty, her blouse torn. He begins to cry.

Inside the room, Pity, The Woman, Jane Bowles, Emily Dickinson and William Harvey hear the sound but think it is gas escaping. The ticker tape spits poems out furiously. They continue reading The Scarlet Letter.

Jane Bowles (*reading*): "Hester Prynne was now fully sensible of the deep injury for which she was responsible to this unhappy man…"

Pity: Bingo.

(*ticker tape*): I'm authentic
        I break my heart all by myself…

Harvey: The heart cannot break.

Emily Dickinson: I cannot live with You—
        It would be Life—
        And Life is over there—
        Behind the shelf.

The Woman: The metaphysics insists upon the singularity of the human soul.

Harvey: (*nodding*) The physics upon the interconnectedness of the heart's chambers.

(*ticker tape*): My secrets cry aloud. I have no need for tongue.
My heart keeps open house. My doors are widely swung.

Jane Bowles (*holding a large bottle of vodka, skips to the door, swings it widely*): Open House!

The stranger enters, wearing a moth helmet. No one notices, except Pity, who, shape shifting, becomes stranger's twin. Jane Bowles falls asleep on their laps.

The Woman gazes at the trio, then picks up The Scarlet Letter *and turning to Harvey and Emily Dickinson, begins to read again.*

The Woman: "Her intellect and heart had their home, as it were in desert places..." (*stops, reads silently ahead, then begins again*): Her scarlet letter was her passport into regions where other women dared not tread..."

Jane Bowles (*waking*): I am the scarlet letter.

Emily Dickinson (*standing, shouting*): You cannot put a Fire out!

The Woman: (*reading louder and louder*) "...Shame, Despair, Solitude! These had been her teachers—stern and wild ones—and they had made her strong, but taught her much amiss."

The Stranger (*setting Jane Bowles carefully down, stands, reads aloud from the ticker tape*): The second after a moth's death there are
One or two hundred other moths...

The Woman (*reading*): "Hester Prynne was now fully sensible of the deep injury for which she was responsible to this unhappy man..."

Pity: Bingo.

(*ticker tape*): She fears him, and will always ask
                What fated her to choose him;
                She meets in his engaging mask
                All reasons to refuse him…

Jane Bowles: But what she meets and what she fears
                Are less than are the downward years
                Down slowly to the foamless weirs
                Of age, were she to lose him…

Pity: Bingo.

Exit Pity and The Stranger. Jane Bowles and The Woman stare at the ticker tape, their faces lit by the poem, which has stopped the tape's flow. The lights fade. The woman throws the stethoscope at the ticker tape and begins to cry. The room fills with the fluttering of moth wings…

Apology

To know nothing   of living things

       Those that exist often

Beside us   Hello, she says

       & does it hear, do you?

Days, nights, watching a stranger's heart

       Stumble against his skin

It wants out, and the body

       Is a flesh dress he'll take off

Only once, at the last

       Hello, she says

Our heart is on exhibit

       Walk around our common institute

Of higher learning

Dark Comedy

—the drift, the solution, all that we float in from time to time
Suddenly transparent, its absolute sheerness, was solid, a thing,
So that dispossession was the outlined shape
Made clear that moment
And momently, from that time, to now—

Everything else is gesture

Everything else is flutter and worry
And her hands in fists her hands
Outstretched in the light
Which highlights the drama—
Not the sheer broken and fluid
Transparency of their
Loss of the other—

Though he says you see I am here
And she says what is you being here now
In the loss of the you I know?
What are you now who are here?

They saw nothing wrong with his heart
In the emergency room
Though there was wrong there

And now, for her, all she can see is drama,
Poetry stripped by time
Where they were lost

Though he says you see I am here

What is your being here now
What are we now who are here
Heart, eye, ear?

Agape, The Woman Is Agape

There could be forgiveness,
If time can be forgiven
Its erasure of human importance

There could be forgiveness,
Or forgetting, which are rumored
To be the same thing

There could be forgiveness,
If forgiveness is a border
As the one I've experienced
Between the living and dead

My dead father shook my foot and I awoke
As I did as a child
And I was again a child

The pity of children is merciless
And in it all is forgiven
Tiny snail in the grass

My father had no hands to touch me
But he did

There could be forgiveness
If love is something invisible that crosses

Continuous Acts

O, heart
In which four different chambers
Help you live and die, continuously
The woman walks around
Chatting, eating—the book is fallen from her hand
She drinks in the beauty of her children's faces
As they change
She herself died
& yet they call her mother
She is now her stranger

Like the Roman baths that fell into decay
As soon as they were privatized,
The woman's period of possession
Is so many pages of antiquity
& only those who love ruins
Love her
She is now her stranger

"It is helpful to visualize the heart as two separate pumps, working
    in series—
Right heart pump, left heart pump. The heart has four chambers,
Two are muscular chambers that propel blood. Two hold the blood
Returning to the heart and at just the right moment, empty."

She is now her stranger, grand inquisitor of the different chambers
To help you live and die continuously.
Are we God or are we a book
Where is our body

Lucy the fossil, The Furies,
Catamite, Sheela na gig, Devi,
    Synonomous with Shatki,
The Baubo, Artemis, Echo, Daphne,
    Armless Venus d'Milo,
Heloise, Helen of Troy, Jeanne d'Arc,
    God the Mother, The Gospel of
Mary, Mary the Mother of God,
    The Rose of Sharon,
Rachel, The Shekinah

The recycled Beloved
Her heart turns to tragedy, turns away
Tragedy is a chamber where she dies continuously, living
The ruin moving through time

Our little girl draws hearts throughout my notebook,
The shapes irregular, elongated down the page,
Much like an actual human heart
Which is shaped more like an upside
Down pear than a valentine.
Her letters likewise do not recognize the constraints of space,
Nor know margins as she writes them from left to right
The stick people she draws
Are all the same size.
Perhaps they are the first God,
The mother-father, matro-pater,
Before they separated
And she was locked in a safe.
Your betrayal thus is historical, and inevitable.
Likewise (or thus inevitably) the woman
Has misplaced the God in herself
What is lost cannot be kind

The woman in time is always
Written out of the creation
This appears to be a function of economy
Or her participation in an economy
That is designed to reduce her
By the year 200, she has many times been excised from divinity
In 1977, the year I graduated from high school,
Pope Paul VI again declared
That a woman couldn't be a priest
Because "Our" lord was a man

"… Right heart pump, left heart pump…
And at just the right moment, empty."

Her spiritual exile is physical

During phase one,
The tube-like heart
Is much like a fish heart.
The second phase,
With two chambers,
Resembles a frog heart.
The three-chambered phase
Is similar to a snake or turtle heart.
The final four-chambered heart structure
Distinguishes the human heart.

Swim swim, hop hop, slither, and plod.
In the two beat something
Tangential and corrosive
Counter motions

I love my mother and while
My mother is not
Can not be said any longer to resemble a Lona Alice—
In sleep, in many moments—
She is my mother
Mine
Always contains
Not mine

The woman is not a ruin

"The creator, becoming arrogant in spirit, boasted himself over all
Exclaimed: 'I am father and God and above me there is no one.'
 But his mother hearing him speak thus cried out against him
'Do not lie!'"

O, heart, our divinity
Generating, making itself grow,
Seeking itself, finding itself
Mother of, father of,
Sister of, itself,
Son and spouse,
Of itself.

Eternal Direction / Insurrection

Scene: Outside the window, the stranger is lying on the ground, looking at the stars. Pre-Raphaelite moths make a heart pattern around his cerebral cortex. He picks up the stethoscope Harvey has left behind and places it on his temple. He hears nothing, but sees behind his eyes the French statue of Liberty, her blouse torn. He begins to cry.

Continuous Acts

La Liberté,
                         In front of the fight

Shares in time a whore's

                         Torn cloth

                         A scarab beetle

Placed above the heart

                         Of the dead carries

The organ to heaven

                         "Do not stand witness against me,"

Cor ne edito

                         "*Eat not the heart*"

Hippocrates

                         The first to understand

Its machine nature

                         & Jesus and his bleeding shrouds

(Torn cloth)

                         The Western tradition

All the posturing

        Synonyms want a role

In the play:

        Spirit   core   nature   mood   mind

Courage: Take heart

        We shall not desert thee

Pluck and those

        Indicating positions in

The body / story / family romance:

        Center   middle   nucleus   hub

Focal point: "There"

We find our heart

      "Who are you?"   In the top

Heavy mind At core

      Are you a center?   A hub?

      & also the deepest reach?

First knowledge Found   "at bottom"

      In one and in the others? It doesn't matter
                  which others

A nucleus Deceived or sound,

      Where seeing through Us We see the many

Interiors of the mystery?

      Place your fingers on your neck to find the pulse

She is standing	Alone there	Is a crowd	
	She is thinking	Of loneliness	It is a crowd
Which surrounds the feeling		She brings	Solely
	To the people there		What
Is this	Thinking/	Feeling	
	In her temple?	She considers long	
It is a life-	Time	She has tried to lose	
	What she thinks	In the others	
It doesn't matter	*Which others*	That she is	
	In them that	They share a heart	
In that a people	Inherit a mind		
	Which is made	Made!	Rousseau!
Poor Rousseau	He too	Alone on his island	

              Come back Rousseau !   Bring your rabbits

Liberté loves   She is pulsing   In our Temple

        The scarab   Pushes the setting

sun overhead   Is it time   To bury mother?

Do they love mother?

        Have we loved   Our mother enough in our

Torn clothes? Look she is alone   She has loved too many

They have taken off her garments Picked up a rock

Endless birth   A statue   On a stage

(HIS)torical Heart

Is an open hole

                Three fingers and a thumb

Ibn al-Nafis disproving Galen

                "There are no holes in the heart"

The physician has removed

                The mitral annulus

 Which resembles a cross

                It's easy to see the logic

Why it's right there!

                Our heart in the crossbow

And so an anatomist

                At a lectern above a corpse

Among students and gawkers

                The subjective ruined opening

Up all around them

Scene 7

The Woman and Jane Bowles have grown tired of The Scarlet Letter, *and are rummaging about the floor, looking for a book to better amuse them. Pity, William Harvey and the Stranger are asleep, and moths rise and fall with their breaths. The Woman picks up Kate Chopin's* The Awakening *looking quizzically at Jane, who looks skeptical but nods.*

The Woman: "A feeling of exultation overtook her, as if some power of significant import had been given her to control the working of her body and her soul. She grew daring and reckless, overestimating her strength. She wanted to swim far out, where no woman had swum before."

Jane Bowles throws herself on the stage floor, pretending to swim. Emily Dickinson, sitting at a table, throws her a pair of flippers, which Jane Bowles puts on and continues to swim.

Emily Dickinson: So stay inside. That's fiction for you…(*yawns*)

Jane Bowles (*looking up from the floor in mid-stroke*): Everything is fiction!

Emily Dickinson (*sternly*): The Soul selects her own Society— / Then—shuts the door—.

Jane Bowles (*swimming more slowly now*): I dreamt I climbed upon a cliff/My sister's hand in mine…I will always need my sister…

Emily Dickinson (*sniffling a little, though smiling, looking fondly at Jane's drama on the floor*): I've known her—from an ample nation— / Choose one…

The ticker tape spews in rapid succession poems from Oxford World Classic Love Poems *and words strobe around the room, lighting the players' faces as they sleep, or speak, unnoticing. William Harvey kicks in his sleep, repeating "right pump, left...and at the right moment, empty" each time the word "heart" lights upon his face.*

The Woman: "How strange and awful it seemed to stand naked under the sky! How delicious! She looked into the distance, and the old terror flamed up for an instant, then sank again...There was the hum of bees, and the musky odor of pinks filled the air."

She drops the book, and slowly slides to her back on the floor next to Jane Bowles. Emily Dickinson, William Harvey, The Stranger and Pity look at each other, and then at the swimming duo. In single-file they walk to where the women lie, and as if dropping from a boat, slip onto the floor and begin to swim.

FIN

The Practical Fruit, Some Small Piece of It

(for Laura Mullen)

I wore the shred
Of a wedding dress,
The portion from elbow to wrist,
With an elegant covered button.
Only one of my arms was married,
The other quite unwed.
Pieces of sound drew me,
And sights escaping
From the sides of my eyes.
Saint of no day,
      Will you be mine?
Underground river,
      Will you rise up in me?

Mojave Letter

Love, I'm afraid, is Darwinesque
Nothing survives it

You pour my tea every morning
And every night I wake up
My heart in my mouth

We ate red pears the first time in Berkeley
They were so sweet and so
I'm learning to hold myself

The way I wanted you, or anyone
To hold me, and see, I don't even need
A mannequin to break my fall

I'm authentic
I break my heart all by myself

Leonardo, Leonardo

At one and the same time, in one and the same subject, two opposite motions cannot take place, that is, repentance and desire.

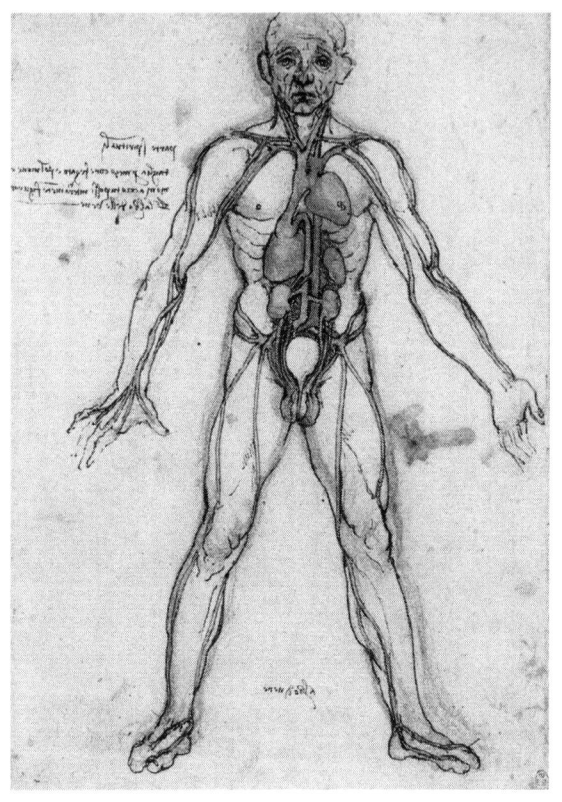

—Leonardo da Vinci's description of the heart

Agape, The Woman Is Agape

But da Vinci is wrong.

At one and the same time,

In the same subject,

There are always at least two motions,

Desire and repentance, love and hate,

Staying home or leaving forever,

Staying home and leaving forever.

Music and silence,

The music in silence,

The silence in music,

The other of Christ,

The other of Hitler,

The women inside the woman,

The strangers inhabiting the man,

The rhythm of the heart,

At the closed center of your eye.

Retrograde Heart

Yes, da Vinci was wrong.

There is the reality of retrograde,
Which is motion in the opposite direction.

And though we are not, love, celestial bodies

Our hearts there do aspire:

swim swim
swim swim

ACKNOWLEDGMENTS

"Continuous Acts," *Women's Studies Quarterly*
"First Acts," "Second Acts" (as "Act 11"), *Free Verse: A Journal of Contemporary Poetry & Poetics.*
"Apology," www.poets.org, *The Academy of American Poets*
"Scene 4" (as "Trobairitz"), *The Ocean State Review*

BARROW STREET POETRY

Unions
Alfred Corn (2014)

O, Heart
Claudia Keelan (2014)

Last Psalm at Sea Level
Meg Day (2014)

This Version of Earth
Soraya Shalforoosh (2014)

Vestigial
Page Hill Starzinger (2013)

You Have to Laugh: New + Selected Poems
Mairéad Byrne (2013)

Wreck Me
Sally Ball (2013)

Blight, Blight, Blight, Ray of Hope
Frank Montesonti (2012)

Self-evident
Scott Hightower (2012)

Emblem
Richard Hoffman (2011)

Mechanical Fireflies
Doug Ramspeck (2011)

Warranty in Zulu
Matthew Gavin Frank (2010)

Heterotopia
Lesley Wheeler (2010)

This Noisy Egg
Nicole Walker (2010)

Black Leapt In
Chris Forhan (2009)

Boy with Flowers
Ely Shipley (2008)

Gold Star Road
Richard Hoffman (2007)

Hidden Sequel
Stan Sanvel Rubin (2006)

Annus Mirabilis
Sally Ball (2005)

A Hat on the Bed
Christine Scanlon (2004)

Hiatus
Evelyn Reilly (2004)

3.14159+
Lois Hirshkowitz (2004)

Selah
Joshua Corey (2003)